THE BUDGETING BEAR

A CHILDREN'S BOOK ABOUT KNOWING WHERE YOUR MONEY IS GOING, STICKING TO A PLAN, AND KNOWING THE DIFFERENCE BETWEEN NEED AND WANT

WRITTEN BY
CHARLOTTE DANE

ILLUSTRATED BY
ADAM RIONG

Bear was amazingly good at resisting temptation. Once he set his budget for the month, he stuck to it, no matter how much he wanted something!

But he knew he only <u>wanted</u> the donut and didn't <u>need</u> it. And it was so small! So he stuck to his normal lunch.

But Bear's cousin agreed to give him his old trombone instead. Since he could save a lot of money and he didn't _need_ the new one, he gladly accepted and wrote a song for him to show his appreciation.

Bear's money habits were admirable. He could always ignore temptations and stick to the budget he made for himself. But he wasn't always like this.

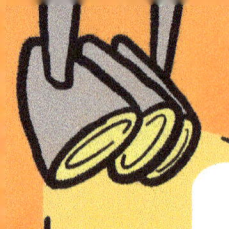

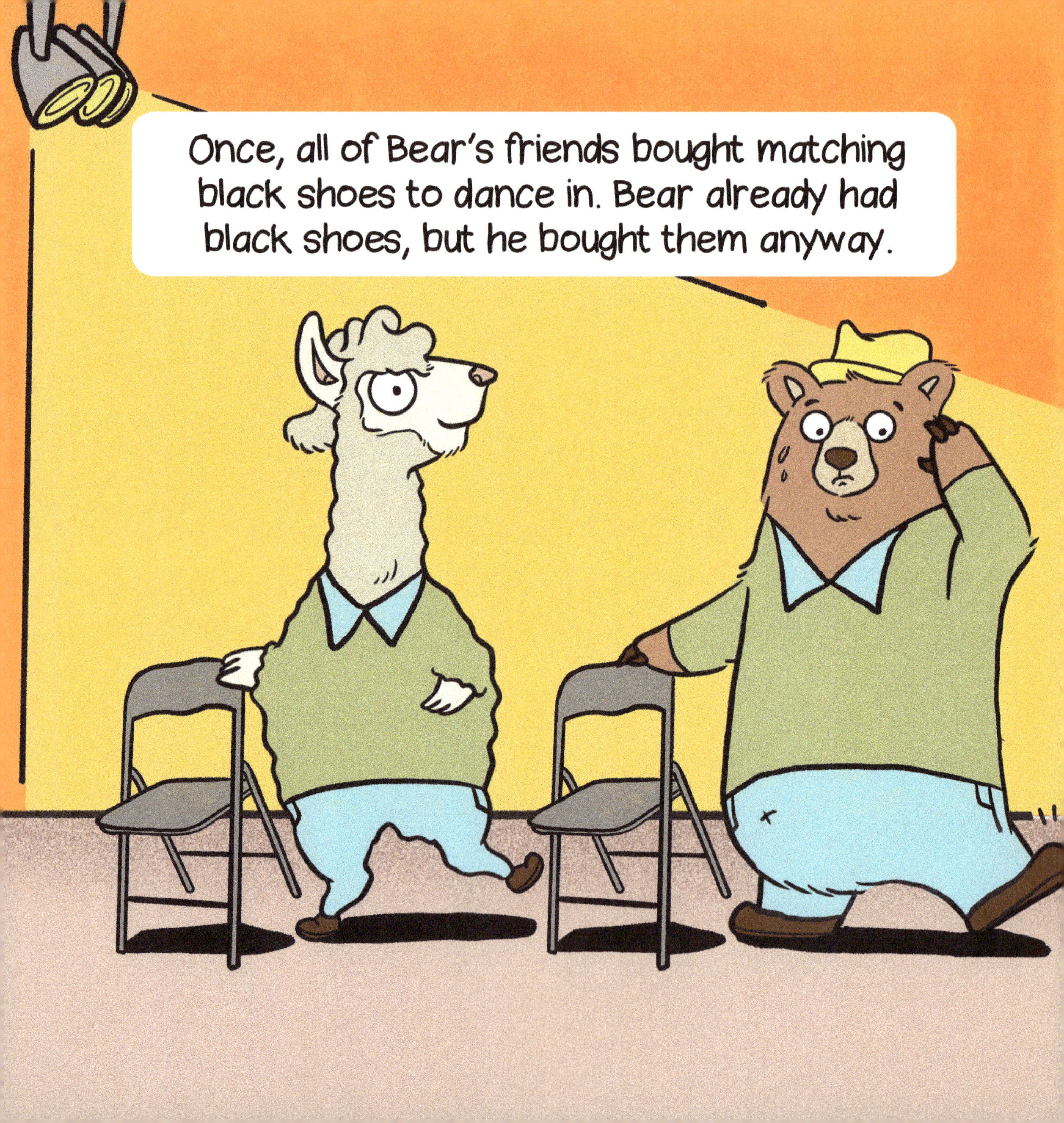
Once, all of Bear's friends bought matching black shoes to dance in. Bear already had black shoes, but he bought them anyway.

He felt great onstage dancing in them, but as soon as the dance was over, he knew he shouldn't have bought them.

Another time, Bear went to an amusement park and bought 5 of the same stuffed animals in different colors just because he could.

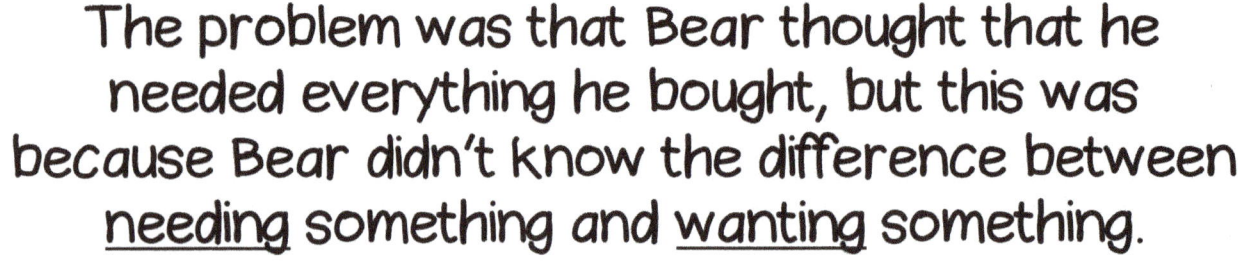

The problem was that Bear thought that he needed everything he bought, but this was because Bear didn't know the difference between <u>needing</u> something and <u>wanting</u> something.

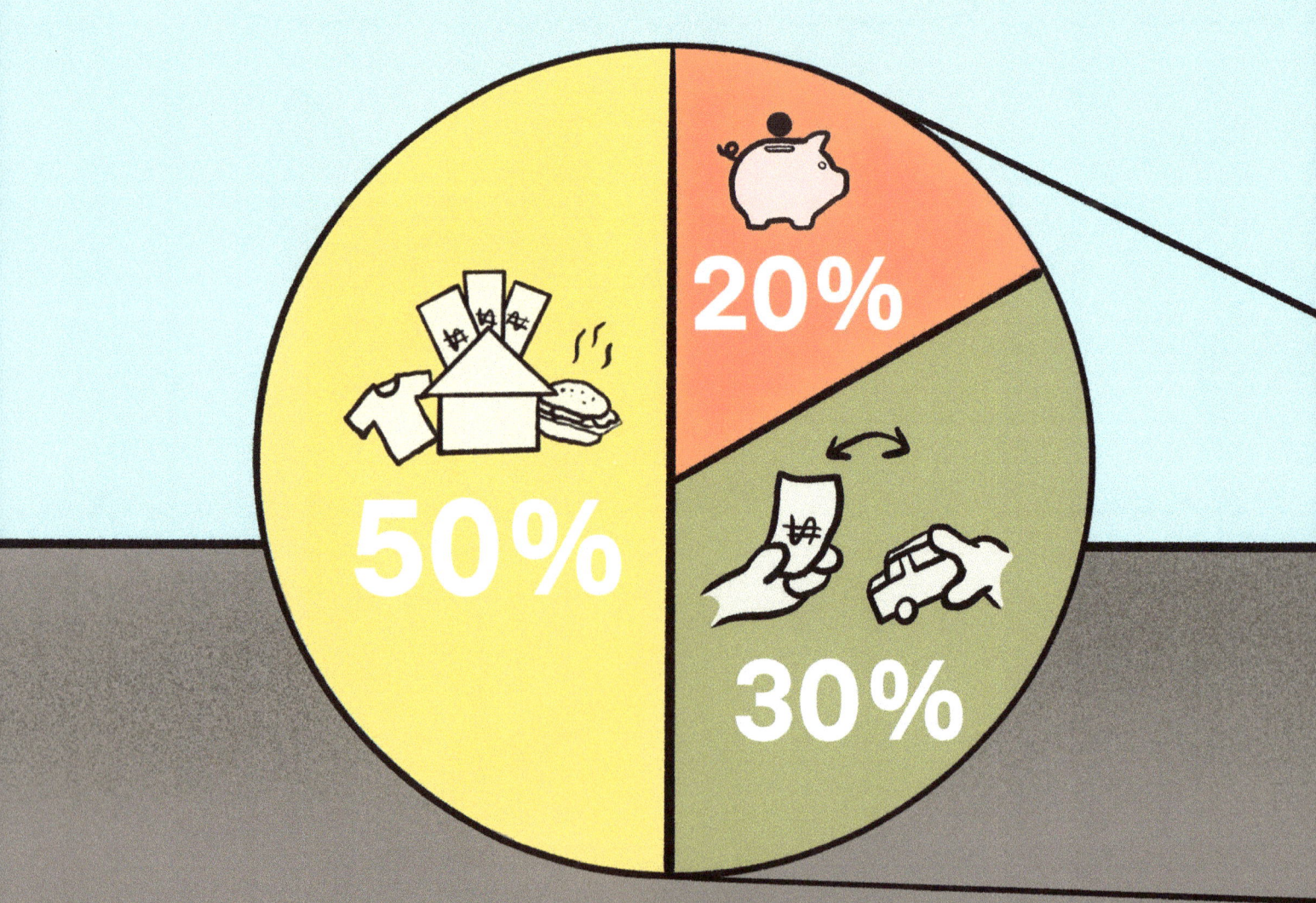

The next week, some of Bear's friends <u>wanted</u> to visit a circus, and some <u>wanted</u> to take a bike ride along the river. This was the perfect time to test his budgeting skills.

Bear still <u>needed</u> new shoes! He went back to the mall and was trying to decide which to buy. Back to the question of <u>need</u> versus <u>want</u>!

He <u>needed</u> shoes that were good for biking, walking, basketball, and video games. He didn't <u>need</u> shoes that were shiny and gold-plated, he only <u>wanted</u> them. Hey, this budgeting thing wasn't so hard!

www.ingramcontent.com/pod-product-compliance
Lightning Source LLC
Chambersburg PA
CBHW042037100526
44587CB00030B/4472